THIS YEAR, NEXT YEAR

by Norah Harding

Playwrights Canada Press
Toronto • Canada

Playwrights Canada Press is the publishing imprint of
the Playwrights Union of Canada (PUC): 54 Wolseley St., 2nd fl.
Toronto, Ontario CANADA M5T 1A5
Tel: (416) 703-0201 Fax: (416) 703-0059
e-mail: cdplays@interlog.com
http://www.puc.ca

Playwrights Canada Press operates with the generous assistance of The Canada Council - Writing and Publishing Section, and Theatre Section, and the Ontario Arts Council.

Cover design by Linda McMaster.
Detail from war poster CN 56-05-12-082, © Canadian War Museum.

Canadian Cataloguing in Publication Data
Norah Harding, 1923 —
This year, next year
A play
ISBN 0-88754-546-7
I. Title.
PS8565.A83T55 1996 C812'.54 C96-931230-X
PR9199.3027M3 1996

First edition: July 1996.
Printed and bound in Winnipeg, Manitoba, Canada.

I dedicate this play to Ben,
my dear mother, and all my sisters.

— Norah Harding

Norah Harding was born in Bournemouth, England. She met and married her husband, a member of the Canadian Army stationed there and came to Canada as a War Bride in 1946 on the *Ile de France*. They settled in her husband's home town of London, Ontario. Norah has been involved with the London Community Players for the past decade, Ingersoll Theatre of Performing Arts, and the Woodstock Little Theatre. She became a professional playwright at the age of 71 when she wrote "This Year, Next Year". Most of the events in the play are factual accounts of her experiences at the time.

PLAYWRIGHT'S FOREWORD

I cannot take sole credit for "This Year, Next Year". It was my great good fortune that it was produced at the Blyth Festival, and that I had the help of Anne Chislett and Janet Amos in the task of bringing my play to performance level. I am eternally grateful to them. Also, I am indebted to my good friends Dale and Pat Bell, who were with me heart and soul throughout, and smoothed the way in innumerable ways.

I think of the triumphant debut of my play as my 'brief, gaudy moment'. It has been a delightful, almost overwhelming experience, but for me the real satisfaction was in being able to bring to life, for all to see, a portrait of my mother, and the courage and steadfastness with which she overcame the adversities which life had dealt her.

— *Norah Harding*

INTRODUCTION BY JANET AMOS

Some years ago, Anne Chislett sent me a script by Norah Harding, entitled "This Year, Next Year". Anne had met Norah while teaching a course in playwriting at Theatre Ontario. Norah had arrived for work with a completed script about her own family set in Bournemouth, England during the final months of World War II. Anne had been immediately impressed with the clarity and depth of characters, the wonderful dialogue, and the potential of the story. I liked the play but, at the time, I was not in a position to produce it.

When I returned to the Blyth Festival in 1994, I found the same script gathering dust on the shelves in my office and, encouraged by Anne, I reread it. But we had no idea where to find Norah after five years. I called information in London, Ontario, her last address, and got a number. A gentle English voice answered the phone. Norah was astonished and delighted that someone finally had an interest in her play and expressed every willingness to start work on it again. Anne Chislett undertook the dramaturgical work on the play, while I directed the workshops and offered encouragement.

It was a unique experience. The biographical nature of the material was a deep source of inspiration. Norah had an uncanny recollection for dialogue and details as well as a profound love of all the characters. Anne set out to help her find a dramatic structure and build in character development which had theatrical power. That involved reordering events and inventing causal connections in the plot to reveal the underlying truth of the story. It was a difficult and delicate process involving weeks of careful, hard work, painful decisions, and endless rewrites. Terry Tweed took over as director in April.

It is always wonderful to discover a new playwright with an obvious and a natural talent. It is even more exciting to discover she has something to say which can strike deep chords of recognition and sympathy with a large, enthusiastic rural audience, such as we have at the Blyth Festival. But the success of "This Year, Next Year" was especially moving because Norah's love for these delightful characters touched and informed everyone who worked on the production. Norah Harding, now at the age of 72, is celebrating her first major success as a playwright. I am sure that this play will be enjoyed by many people in theatres across the country.

Janet Amos
January 15, 1996
Blyth, Ontario

"This Year, Next Year" was first performed at the Blyth Festival in July, 1995 with the following cast.

(in order of appearance)

SHEILAH	*Trish O'Reilly*
IVY	*Deborah Drakeford*
NORAH	*Jacklyn Francis*
MAGGIE	*Barbara Worthy*
AUNT GIRLIE	*Tedde Moore*
UNCLE HARRY	*Harry Booker*

Tim O'Gorman appeared as BEN.

Directed by Terry Tweed.
Assistant director and dramaturg — Anne Chislett.
Set and costume design by Victoria Wallace.
Lighting design by Lesley Wilkinson.
Stage manager — Kathryn Davies.

THE CHARACTERS

MUM (MAGGIE)	age 50
IVY	age 26
NORAH	age 20
SHEILAH	age 18
UNCLE HARRY	age 48
AUNT GIRLIE	age 46

A Canadian soldier appears in the window at the end of the play.

THE SET

The living room of a working-class family in Bournemouth, England, during World War II. The walls are papered in a cheery pattern. The floor is patterned linoleum with two or three Axminster-type rugs. A plain double-sash window in the centre of the back wall has roller-type dark opaque blinds and curtains. There is a coal-burning fireplace with an overmantel shelf. On it are several photos of the family, some of whom are in uniform. Above the mantel is a mirror. There is a large dining-room table with six chairs, four around it, two against walls. Other furniture includes a china cabinet with the Sunday tea service; a sideboard with glasses, a two-tiered cake plate, side plates for example; Mum's shabby but comfortable wing chair; and a table with the wireless radio. An old-fashioned light fixture with a fringed shade hangs at the centre of the room. There are two doors, one to the kitchen which also leads to the backdoor, which everyone uses, and one to the hallway where coats are hung, which also leads to the stairs.

PRODUCTION NOTES

It might be helpful if the programme for this play noted that the date of the Allied Invasion of Europe (D Day) was June 6th, 1944.

Before the play starts, a recording of the latter part of Churchill's "Finest Hour" speech helps to set the mood for the audience.

The following is the text of the broadcast used in the scene change after Act Two, Scene One and continuing into the top of Act Two, Scene Two. Items are drawn from news of that date.

"This is the BBC Home Service. Here is the (time) news with (name of announcer). In daylight raids yesterday, 300 enemy aircraft were launched against London and Southeast England. More than half of the German airplanes were shot down by British forces. Incendiaries were dropped in several districts of London and East Anglia, and a hotel housing Commonwealth troops was destroyed in Bournemouth.

The daylight air warfare was extended to Berlin yesterday when American fighters made a sweep over the capital for the first time, while Fortresses and Liberators bombed German targets. The biggest bombs ever made, 12,000 lb. or five and a third tons, are now being used by the RAF. Originally it was reported that 45 Allied aircraft had been lost. That number is now officially reduced by two.

The third major offensive to be launched by Germany in an attempt to drive the Fifth Army from the Anzio beach head is now described as a costly failure. Severe losses were inflicted on the enemy by the Allied artillery. Lieutenant-General Mark Clark has sent a message of congratulations to the commanding general of the Allied forces in the Mediterranean.

The Ministry of Labour has carried out another half-yearly inquiry into the actual earnings of more than six million workpeople in the manufacturing industries. Earnings are 76 percent higher than in 1938. The Prime Minister, this morning, revealed that the War Cabinet has agreed "not to exclude from their discussions" the renewed demand for increased service pay and allowances, which provoked a heated debate in Parliament last week.

Lady Violet Bonham-Carter has agreed to accept nomination as President of the Liberal party organisation to succeed the late Lord Menton. This marks the first time that a woman has been proposed as president of the party.

The Princess Royal, attended by the Dowager Lady Lloyd, today visits Red Cross depots at Menston, Baildon, Shipley and Bingley."

***

It is left to the director's discretion as to how much of this report to use.

Trish O'Reilly (l), Jacklyn Francis (c), and Barbara Worthy (r) in the 1995 Blyth Festival production.
— photo by James Hockings, Off Broadway Photography, London.

Act One, Scene One

A Sunday afternoon, mid-February, 1944.

A rug and two chairs have been pushed aside. The wireless is tuned to the American Forces Network - AFN, and one of the Big Bands is playing, but not loudly. SHEILAH, a lively eighteen-year-old, is enthusiastically jitterbugging to a tune such as "Chattanooga Choo Choo," or "Little Brown Jug". IVY, twenty-six, with the air of someone no longer interested in life, is knitting.

SHEILAH Come on, Ivy. Have a go.

IVY No, thanks.

SHEILAH Oh, Ive, come on.

IVY I said no thanks.

SHEILAH I don't believe you mean that. All the dances you used to go to? Who was the first one out there when they played the tango? Who did the exhibition rumba? Who won the quick-step competition at the pavillion?

IVY I worked overtime every day this week. I just want to have a quiet Sunday.

SHEILAH Anyone would think it was a sin to enjoy yourself. Come on. *(pulling IVY up)* Listen to the beat. Let's go.

IVY Look, if you want to dance, dance. But leave me out of it. *(SHEILAH spins out and knocks over a chair)* Sheilah! Watch it.

SHEILAH There's no space in here, and that stupid table-shelter takes up all the front room.

IVY Thank your lucky stars we've never needed it.

SHEILAH *(going to her again)* Please, Ive.

IVY I said "No." *(she turns off the radio)* You know what a light sleeper Mum is.

SHEILAH Oh, yes. She "never sleeps a wink". Funny, the noises she makes sound suspiciously like snoring.

IVY Sheilah!

SHEILAH Look, Mum would be pleased if you were dancing. You know she would. *(IVY goes back to her knitting)* Go on, pretend you didn't hear me, but you practically promised her you'd go to the camp dance with me.

IVY I only said I'd think about it.

SHEILAH Well, think about it. All those big American bands, Glenn Miller and all that lot — like we've seen them in the films...it's smashing! And Ivy, twenty men for every girl! Wow!

IVY I'm glad you're finding the war so enjoyable.

SHEILAH And now there's all these Americans — just dying to find a girl to spend their money on!

IVY *(bitterly)* Don't forget that's what a lot of them will be doing. Just dying.

SHEILAH Well, don't look at me. The war wasn't my idea.

IVY I didn't say it was, but...

SHEILAH At least some of us are trying to cheer them up — going to the dances, Ivy.

IVY Oh, yes. And some girls have been so good at cheering them up, they're pushing prams now.

SHEILAH Correct me if I'm wrong, but I don't think dancing caused their condition.

IVY All the same, I don't want some GI's hands all over me. I'm staying home.

SHEILAH Oh, please, Ive. I can't go if you don't. Mum won't let me go alone.

The gate latch clicks. NORAH goes by the window.

Here's our Norah back. She'll tell you how great the dances are.

IVY Then why has she stopped going?

SHEILAH It's this new boyfriend of hers. She's out with him every night now.

IVY It won't last.

SHEILAH That's what I reckon.

IVY He'll soon bite the dust the same as the others.

NORAH *(entering happily)* Where's Mum?

SHEILAH Upstairs.

NORAH heads towards the stairs.

IVY Where do you think you're going?

NORAH I just want to ask Mum something.

IVY She's trying to get a bit of rest, like the doctor told her to. How much do you think she got last night with those blasted sirens?

NORAH There weren't sirens...were there?

IVY You slept through them, as usual. Mum was up four times.

NORAH Oh...well, I'll just see if she's awake.

IVY What's so important you can't wait till she comes down?

SHEILAH *(after a pause)* Yes, what is it?

NORAH Oh...nothing. *(taking off her coat and head-scarf, dreamily, with a half-smile)* Gosh, it isn't half cold out.

SHEILAH Funny! You look all warm and rosy, doesn't she, Ive? *(to NORAH)* Got your love to keep you warm?

NORAH Did you know the damp here makes it seem colder than Canada?

SHEILAH How interesting.

NORAH *(oblivious to the teasing, happy to have an audience)* And we don't dress for the weather like they do.

IVY Like who do?

NORAH Canadians. They have chamois linings in their coats.

SHEILAH Are you alluding to Canadian's coats in general? Or just one particular Canadian's coat?

NORAH Oh, you. You know very well I'm talking about Ben.

SHEILAH turns on the radio. The music is "In the Mood".

SHEILAH Ooh. *(grabbing her)* They're playing our favourite. Come on.

NORAH Sheilah!

But NORAH gets into the dance. The girls put on a good show, but suddenly the station's jammed.

NORAH They've jammed it again.

IVY Those damn Nazis.

SHEILAH But we were really going to town there. Norah, come with me tonight. Let's show'em how it's done.

NORAH I've sort of lost interest in dances.

SHEILAH Please...I don't want to have to stay home.

NORAH I thought Ivy was going with you?

IVY I never said that.

SHEIALH She's got the idea that camp dances are the next thing to Sodom and Gomorrah!

IVY Well, aren't they?

NORAH Well...

IVY I knew it.

NORAH Sometimes they get — well — a bit out of hand. There's a lot of drinking goes on, and if you're not careful...but it's not altogether the GIs' fault. Some women — well! They go to the dances to get hold of some poor soldier just for what they can get out of him! Cigarettes, candy...and they don't care what they have to do for it! So the boys think we're all the same...well, some of them...the trouble is, they don't know which are which, and we don't know which are which...see what I mean?

IVY Clear as mud.

NORAH So me and Sheilah play it safe and never go outside with anyone.

SHEILAH Actually, it was after I saw Norah going off with this wolf that we made that rule!

NORAH He was going to get me some Hershey bars from the P.X.

SHEILAH Before you got the wrapper off, he'd have got your knickers off.

NORAH I know now I was stupid — but they're such fast talkers!

SHEILAH You have to learn to talk fast yourself — or you'd end up like the girl who talked so slow that...

IVY *(joining in with SHEILAH))*...before she could say she wasn't that kind of a girl...

NORAH *(joining in so that all three finish the line)* ...she was! Ha! Ha! *(remembering a joke)* Tell Ivy about that one Joycey Williams went out with.

SHEILAH Oh yes! Such a gentleman! So grateful to Joycey for going out with him, he said, that he'd brought her a present. It was a pair of those new nylon stockings! Imagine! He asked her if she liked them, and then gave her one to look at. She was ecstatic! Nylon stockings! Any girl'd give her eye-teeth for a pair.

NORAH I know I would!

SHEILAH "Oh yes," she said, - "they're ever so nice!" "Well," he said, "you be ever so nice to me tonight, and I'll give you the other one."

IVY Creep. What did she say?

SHEILAH She didn't say a word. She just walked away, real fast, into the blackout, and left him with his mouth open - and just one stocking!

IVY Well, you know what our boys say. The only thing wrong with the Americans is that they're over sexed, over paid, and over here!

NORAH But our boys are no angels either.

SHEILAH No, we fought for our honour a few times! Remember the Lancashire Fusiliers!

NORAH The Hampshires!

SHEILAH The Regiment La Chaudiere!

NORAH The Scottish Highlanders! The Free French!

SHEILAH And what about the Canucks?

NORAH Sheilah!

SHEILAH Oh, I'm sorry. They're different, aren't they, Norah?

NORAH I really couldn't say, not having met them all, but if you are alluding to Ben...

SHEILAH *(groaning)* Here we go again!

NORAH But Ben's different. Really he is.

SHEILAH We've heard that before, haven't we, Ive?

IVY Only about fifty times!

NORAH That's not true!

SHEILAH For a start, what about Walter, the one from Yorkshire, who spent all his free time propping up our wall, waiting for a glimpse of you?

NORAH He was just someone I liked to dance with.

SHEILAH And that sergeant in The Black Watch who wanted to take you up to Scotland to meet his mother?

IVY And that P.T. Instructor who used to bring his men past our house on their morning run — so that he could dash in with messages for you!

SHEILAH Left them running on the spot outside!

IVY Mum soon put a stop to that!

SHEILAH He was a handsome devil. I fancied him myself!

NORAH *(laughing)* All right! I admit it! I had a crush on one or two, but that was before Ben.

SHEILAH I can't understand you! This Canadian's not even good-looking!

NORAH *(indignantly)* Looks aren't everything! He's got a — a sincere face.

SHEILAH And he's a lousy dancer!

NORAH Are you saying that I shouldn't marry him because he can't do the tango?

IVY Marry him? Good God!

NORAH *(radiant)* I didn't mean to tell you yet. I wanted Mum to be the first to know. We were walking through Meyrick Park and he...proposed.

SHEILAH Did he go down on one knee? In the middle of all the Sunday strollers?

NORAH Of course not.

SHEILAH What did he say? *(acting it out)* "Say you'll be mine or I'll kill mysclf?"

NORAH If you really want to know, he said, "Do you think you could put up with me for the rest of your life?"

SHEILAH I should never have let you wear my blouse today. It's just too sexy!

NORAH *(sighing)* I know. *(beat)* Oh, just think! I'll be going to Canada! And guess what?! Ben lives in London, only this one's in — oh, what did he say? Oh — the province of Ontario.

IVY Do you mean you said "Yes?"

NORAH Oh, yes!

SHEILAH Why ever did you do that?

NORAH Oh, Sheilah...how can you ask? Don't you remember how we used to lie in bed planning our wedding days? How we'd dreamed about floating down the aisle...all satin and lace...and roses and orange blossoms...with everyone throwing confetti? The organ pealing out "The Wedding March" and the bells ringing.

IVY If the bells ring now, Norah, it means the Germans have landed.

SHEILAH *(laughing)* Yes, you'd better forget all that kid stuff and come back down to earth.

NORAH You can laugh all you like. It's still my dream. And now it's complete. Now I've got the bridegroom.

IVY It's going to be an awful let-down for him when you tell him you've changed your mind.

NORAH You think I'm going to change my mind?

IVY I hope you will.

NORAH Well, you can hope all you like, but I meant it when I said "Yes". Ben's just wonderful! I'll never change my mind.

IVY shakes her head.

SHEILAH I wouldn't want to make book on that, sister dear. What about the pact we made, you and I? Remember — the two musketeers? We were going to stick together, though thick and thin, hell or high water, until the war was over, and stay in our single state.

NORAH I know.

SHEILAH "Eat, drink, and be merry," we said, "because the next bomb may have our names on it!"

NORAH Wait until you meet someone you really care about.

SHEILAH You know very well I've got someone. Charlie! He's dead keen to get married. *(sighing)* I'd marry him tomorrow, only...

NORAH Only what?

SHEILAH He's a fighter pilot, isn't he? Just finished one tour of Ops, and all geared up for the next. According to statistics the odds on his coming out of this alive are one in three...Anyway I don't want to be tied down.

NORAH And that's all right with him?

SHEILAH He sees things my way most of the time. He agrees the wedding can wait till the war's over.

IVY That's what I call sensible.

SHEILAH Except he's dead keen on having the honeymoon now.

IVY Sheilah!

NORAH *(at the same time)* Sheilah!

SHEILAH So far I've been able to make him behave, but only just. The trouble is, deep down, I don't really want him to...*(She gets an idea.)* That's what you ought to do...

NORAH What?

SHEILAH Just go off with Ben and have a dirty weekend. Get it out of your system.

NORAH Sheilah! I don't understand you sometimes.

SHEILAH If you really don't, what do you want to get married for?

NORAH Stop making a joke of everything! Look, I'm relying on you and Ivy for support.

IVY For what?

SHEILAH I thought you were all set.

NORAH As far as Ben and I are concerned, yes...but.. there's all this red tape from the Canadian Army!

SHEILAH What has the Canadian Army got to do with it?

NORAH I have to be inspected, if you please — to make sure I'm fit to be a Canadian's wife. Ben says their padre will want a little chat with me, to see if I'm of good character! Look me over as if I was a...a horse for sale!

SHEILAH Well, you're sound of wind and limb, got good fetlocks, and your teeth are quite decent.

NORAH *(exasperated with SHEILAH for taking things so lightly)* I'm glad you find it all so amusing!

SHEILAH Oh, for heaven's sake, Norah, where's your sense of humour!

NORAH Then I have to have a blood test. What for, I don't know!

IVY It's to make sure you haven't got VD.

NORAH Oh.

SHEILAH Or any other of those sociable diseases.

NORAH It makes it seem so— *(makes a face)*

SHEILAH Cheer up, that's one test you're sure to pass.

NORAH I haven't told you the worst part. Even after all the forms are filled out, we still have to wait three months. Ben says it's to give us time to think it over seriously. Three months!

IVY I don't see how you can quarrel with that.

NORAH But I don't want to wait. Once Mum's signed the paper and Ben gives it to his C.O., they should let us go ahead right away.

IVY Paper? What paper? What would Mum be signing?

NORAH Oh, this form. *(she takes a paper from her purse or pocket and passes it to IVY)* Ben had it with him...hoping I'd say yes.

SHEILAH Most men offer a diamond ring.

IVY *(looking at the paper)* You need your parents' consent?

NORAH Just Mum's signature.

SHEILAH You mean you can't get married unless Mum agrees?

NORAH *(nodding)* Because I'm not twenty-one yet.

IVY Well, that's that.

SHEILAH You haven't got a prayer.

NORAH I know my going off to Canada may be a bit of a shock, but I'm sure she'll like Ben.

IVY Mum's never going to sign that paper.

SHEILAH You didn't think she would, did you? You must be daft.

IVY The last thing she wants is for you to marry a service-man!

NORAH *(alarmed)* Well, I mean...if you two back me up...you know...especially you, Ivy. She'll listen to you. I know she will.

IVY Me?

SHEILAH Norah, forget it. And speaking of forgetting, when I lent you that blouse, you promised to press my skirt, didn't you?

NORAH Oh, Sheilah, I've more important things to think about...

SHEILAH Fine. You can iron while you're thinking.

NORAH Sheilah!

SHEILAH *(exiting)* I'll get it for you.

NORAH *(turning to IVY)* Ivy...you can understand how I feel, can't you? After all, you and Reg...

IVY Don't! There's no comparison. We were sweethearts even at school! You haven't known this Canadian five minutes.

NORAH Do you have to call him "this Canadian"? His name's Ben. And I've known him six weeks!

IVY Norah, you and — Ben — are acting like a couple of fools!

NORAH But...if you had it to do over, you'd marry Reg again, wouldn't you?

NORAH holds IVY's gaze until IVY turns away.

IVY I don't know.

NORAH Oh, Ivy...

IVY Look, the war can't last much longer. Be sensible. Wait till it's over!

SHEILAH enters with the skirt.

NORAH Please, I promised Ben I'd have that paper all signed, and give it back to him this evening. Don't let me down. Help me. Please!

IVY *(shaking her head)* Sorry.

NORAH Sheilah...?

SHEILAH I'm with Ivy. Forget it. Now, I want my skirt for the dance. Get a move on. Mum'll be getting up any minute.

NORAH Maybe if I have tea all ready it will put her in a good mood.

SHEILAH Tea's not going to do it. You should put out the sherry instead.

NORAH I'm going to get Mum to say yes — with or without your help. *(slight pause)* At least you could set the table for me.

SHEILAH *(ungraciously)* Oh, all right

NORAH *(humbly)* Ivy, will you cut the bread and butter. I can't cut it thin like you.

IVY *(making a helpless gesture)* You remember that Uncle Harry and Aunt Girlie are coming to tea?

NORAH Aunt Girlie? Oh, I'd forgotten...

SHEILAH It's nearly a year since they were here, isn't it? Last Easter.

IVY *(she loathes Aunt Girlie)* We'll be seeing a lot of Girlie now they've moved back to Bournemouth. *(exits to the kitchen)*

NORAH Still, Mum'll be happy to have Uncle Harry close again, won't she?

SHEILAH I wonder if Aunt Girlie's changed at all?

MUM appears in the hall doorway, startling them when she speaks.

MUM What was that about your Aunt Girlie?

NORAH *(sweetly)* Oh Mum, you're up! Did you have a nice rest?

MUM I didn't sleep a wink. And my head...

NORAH *(eager to please)* Shall I get you a couple of aspirins?

MUM No, don't bother. I'll be all right once I get a cup of tea. What were you saying about your Aunt Girlie?

NORAH Nothing, Mum.

SHEILAH Nothing at all.

MUM Well, just you watch how you talk about your aunt. I didn't bring you up to be disrespectful to your elders.

SHEILAH We didn't say anything.

NORAH *(brightly)* Tea's nearly ready, and Ivy's doing the bread and butter.

MUM Well, it's nice to know someone's got a bit of thought.

SHEILAH What about me? I'm setting the table, aren't I? *(picking up her skirt and thrusting it at NORAH, as she hisses)* Get on with it!

NORAH *(grabbing the skirt, and nodding to SHEILAH distractedly)* Shall I put the kettle on, Mum?

MUM *(sharply)* Just look at that mat! And those chairs! I go upstairs for five minutes for a bit of peace and quiet, and you girls turn the place upside down!

MUM bends over to straighten the mat just as NORAH rushes over to do the same. They bang heads.

NORAH *(dismayed)* Ooh! Sorry, Mum! *(she straightens rug and chairs)* Anything else I can do, Mum?

MUM You can get a pot of my plum jam from my store-cupboard. It's your uncle's favourite.

NORAH *(fervently)* Oh, everybody loves your jam, Mum. *(starting for the kitchen.)*

MUM Put it out in the cut-glass dish, mind!

NORAH Yes, Mum.

MUM And fill the kettle right up!

SHEILAH *(behind MUM's back, mouthing to NORAH)* Iron — my — skirt!

MUM And don't forget to warm the teapot!

Exiting backwards as she shakes her head "No" to MUM and nodding her head "Yes" to SHEILAH, and smiling at MUM all the time, NORAH backs into the door frame quite hard, but maintains her smile nevertheless as she disappears into the kitchen.

MUM What ever's the matter with that girl?! She's acting like an idiot! *(calls to kitchen)* And cut the sponge into eight!

We hear the gate-latch click, and SHEILAH and MUM look towards the window. HARRY and GIRLIE pass by, on their way to the back door. AUNT GIRLIE is wearing a very large, hairy fur coat in which she resembles a walking haystack.

MUM And, Sheilah, mind you say "No" when the sponge cake is passed for the second time. The extra slices are for the guests.

SHEILAH Yes, Mum.

MUM And go easy on the sugar. One teaspoon's ample. Our ration doesn't go very far these days.

IVY *(bringing in the bread and butter and the cake)* Norah's making the tea.

We hear HARRY and GIRLIE enter offstage, greeting NORAH. GIRLIE and HARRY enter, GIRLIE leading the way. She plants herself front and centre, as if in a spotlight, anticipating the comments on her new fur coat. She waits expectantly. HARRY stands quietly to the side. The family is rendered speechless by the sight of her.

MUM *(after a pause, feebly)* Well, here you are then.

GIRLIE *(beaming)* Yes, here we are! *(waiting expectantly.)* Hallo, Sheilah. My, your hair has got red.

HARRY smiles and nods to the girls.

SHEILAH Hallo, Auntie Girlie, Uncle Harry.

GIRLIE And how are you, Ivy, you poor thing! *(to MUM, shaking her head)* My, but she's not looking good, is she, Maggie?

IVY *(muttering)* Hello.

GIRLIE And what about you, Maggie? I said to Dinger, what with the war dragging on and worryin' about poor Ivy, I doubt if Maggie's heart'll stand up to it.

MUM As a matter of fact, I'm feeling much better these days, Girlie. I took the doctor's advice and packed in my job.

HARRY Maggie, that's good news.

GIRLIE Well, I thought you'd be slavin' away in that laundry until you dropped.

NORAH *(entering with the teapot, and brushing past GIRLIE, who is blocking the way)* Excuse me, Auntie Girlie.

MUM No need to ask how you are, Girlie. You're looking very well. But let me look at you, Harry...I think you've lost some weight. You had the 'flu Christmas time, didn't you? How do you feel now?

HARRY Yes, well, I'm not—

GIRLIE *(cutting him off as usual)* He's all right, Maggie! You know how men baby themselves if they're a bit off-colour! You're fine, aren't you Dinger! *(as HARRY nods, she smirks at them all)* I suppose I should say he will be fine — when he gets over the shock of what this fur coat cost!

MUM *(with double meaning)* It must have been a lot!

GIRLIE Well, Maggie, as I always say, if you want the best, you've got to pay for it! You know me!

MUM *(flatly)* Yes.

NORAH *(quickly)* It's ever so nice, Aunt Girlie.

GIRLIE, pleased, stands, front centre, simpering.

MUM Are we going to stand here all day then? The tea will be stewed. Ivy, take your Aunt and Uncle's things, and hang them up.

HARRY hands IVY his 'mac'.

GIRLIE I'd better keep my coat on. I feel the damp so.

IVY exits with HARRY's 'mac'.

SHEILAH *(mischievously)* Do you know the damp here makes it seem colder than Canada?

NORAH looks daggers at her.

GIRLIE Canada?

MUM What's Canada got to do with anything?

NORAH Nothing at all.

SHEILAH It's just something people say.

GIRLIE I heard a fine old tale about Canada, Maggie — our butcher was telling me. His niece got mixed up with one of those Canadian airmen. He told her about the big ranch he had — thousands of acres — in some place named Detroit. Well, she thought she'd struck it lucky. Told her he'd marry her, after the war, and take her back there! Cosying up to her, he was. She fell for it hook, line, and sinker! Lucky for her, one of his mates let the cat out the bag. Not only was it a pack of lies, but he already had a wife into the bargain! Imagine.

SHEILAH You don't know if this Detroit is anywhere near the Canadian version of London, do you, Aunt Girlie?

GIRLIE I don't know and I don't want to know. I hope I've got more sense than to go traipsin' off to a Godforsaken place like Canada. Give me good old England any day, damp and all. A good coal fire'll soon get rid of it.

MUM The way coal's rationed, we can't have much of a one these days.

GIRLIE We're never short of coal! Those old Tories see to that. They like their club nice and warm, and of course, they've got the money all right, eh, Dinger? *(as HARRY opens his mouth to answer, she goes straight on)* Best thing we ever did was when we saw the light and became Conservatives!

MUM *(as IVY returns to the room)* Fix the blackout while you're up, Ivy, or we'll have Mr. Robbins after us.

IVY does so. MUM has been pouring the tea and passing it round.

GIRLIE *(pityingly)* Of course, all these old houses are damp and draughty. I suppose you're used to it, and it is cheap rent.

MUM This house suits me just fine, thank you, Girlie.

GIRLIE I wonder you can even still afford this, now you're not working. Course, Maggie, you did bring it on your own head, didn't you?

HARRY Girlie!

GIRLIE *(unheeding)* You had a nice little pension when Madge and Ivy 's father was lost at sea — a nice little naval pension's not to be sneezed at...

MUM That's water under the bridge, Girlie.

GIRLIE And you lost it all when you married that good-for-nothing Irishman.

NORAH reacts to this.

HARRY Girlie!

MUM Norah, pass the jam to your uncle.

GIRLIE *(intercepting it)* Oh, thanks. *(returning to her theme)* Yes, the only thing he did for you before he ran off was leave you two more mouths to feed! *(shaking her head)*

MUM That's all in the past. With the three girls bringing home a pay packet we're managing just fine.

GIRLIE Ah, but you won't always have'em, will you? Well, you'll have Ivy, I suppose. *(giving a pitying look to IVY who is biting her tongue, but remains silent)* But I expect Nooie and Sheilah'll be getting married one of these days, eh?

SHEILAH *(looking at NORAH)* I'm going to get a bit of fun out of life first.

GIRLIE How about you, Nooie?

NORAH *(changing the subject)* Aunt Girlie, what was it that made you change your politics? Was it Winston Churchill?

GIRLIE *(mystified)* Eh?

NORAH Was it Winston Churchill? I mean, you used to be Liberals, didn't you? Before you moved back, didn't you and Uncle Harry look after the Liberal Club?

GIRLIE Oh! That's what you're meaning is it ? *(chuckles)* No, Nooie, Conservative, Liberal, Labour — it don't make no difference. The Tories offered us a nice little flat over the club, a nice little job for Dinger, running the bar, an' a bit extra for me, doin' the caterin' for their socials! Politics, Nooie, is knowing which side your bread's buttered on. That's all. And the sooner you learn that the better off you'll be. See?

NORAH *(obviously bewildered)* Oh...yes.

MUM Seems to me, Girlie, it's that kind of thinking that gave Hitler his start. Principles are still important, to my way of thinking.

GIRLIE For them that can afford 'em. But nobody would expect you, in your position, to worry about principles.

IVY I've noticed some people aren't worrying at all. Some people seem to think that the war is just for their benefit.

An awkward pause

SHEILAH *(enjoying this)* Er...shall I pass the cake, Mum?

MUM Yes, of course. *(discovering an empty pot)* Norah, you didn't fill the tea pot right up.

NORAH Oh...sorry.

SHEILAH Dreaming of sincere faces again?

NORAH The kettle should still be hot. *(going off with the teapot, she thumps SHEILAH on the back as she passes her)*

GIRLIE *(with a mouthful of sponge)* Better add a bit more tea too, Nooie, or it'll be too weak to come out the pot. We don't want to be drinking no cricket's piddle!

MUM When you use a good tea, like my Typhoo Tips, you can always get a decent second cup, Girlie. Now, Harry, are you still fire watching, even after that flu?

HARRY I have to do my bit...

GIRLIE I tried to stop him, Maggie. At his age, out in all weathers...I said if he had to volunteer, why not look for something that might do us a bit of good.

NORAH returns.

MUM A man doesn't think that way when there's a war on. Or a woman either. All my girls are working at something that'll help the war effort, and doing a six day week. Sheilah's with the Ministry of Information, and Ivy's on shift work at that aircraft factory.

GIRLIE Ah, but think of the money you're makin', Ive! Twice as much as in that old office, I'll bet!

IVY I'm not doing it for the money. I hate the job, but perhaps it'll help shorten this rotten war!

MUM That's what we're all praying for.

NORAH My firm's making fittings for landing craft. We're ever so busy.

HARRY I'm not surprised. All the talk these days is about the invasion of Europe.

MUM I'm tired of all the talk about the invasion. Let's have some action.

HARRY Well, it's no secret it's going to be some time this summer...*(to NORAH)* The rivers around here are choked with your landing craft.

NORAH This summer?

MUM They've said that for thc last two summers, Harry. I'll believe it when it happens.

HARRY This time it will, Maggie. You'll see. Italy's thrown in the towel, and the Nazis are on the run everywhere. The Russians are killing them off like flies. I tell you, "we've finally come to the beginning of the end."

IVY Don't forget it'll be the end for thousands of the troops that have to hit those beaches first, Uncle Harry.

HARRY That's true. Like those poor Canadians at Dieppe.

IVY We don't hear much talk about that, do we?

GIRLIE Red with blood the English Channel will be! Red with blood!

MUM Girlie, don't. I can't bear to think of it.

HARRY Well, Maggie, you've got to face facts. What do you think all these Americans and Australians and Canadians and Free French and the rest of them are here for?

NORAH *(dismay in her voice)* Do you really think it'll be this summer, Uncle Harry?

HARRY Oh, it has to be, Nooie.

GIRLIE You sound worried, Nooie? Got a boyfriend, then?

MUM Norah's always got a boyfriend or two hanging around!

GIRLIE Like my Sylvie. Right now there's a big ship in at Poole Harbour—

HARRY Mentioning no names—

GIRLIE I wasn't—

HARRY Remember...'Loose lips sink ships!'

GIRLIE I know, I know. "Be like Dad, — keep Mum," eh? Well, as I was saying, there's my Sylvie — can't move for one or the other officers asking her out. I suppose she'll end up like our Reeny — married to an officer too!

HARRY Let our Sylvie make up her own mind.

GIRLIE Of course — my Sylvie being a beauty queen — well, she can just about pick and choose! But what a little madam she is! I've spoiled her, I suppose! She just won't wear utility! Oh, not that you girls look that bad in utility, but it's nothing but the best for my Sylvie. Paid ten pound for a pair of suede shoes the other day.

Satisfied, she helps herself to more cake.

NORAH *(impressed)* Gosh — three pound's my limit!

SHEILAH Never mind, Norah. I'm sure someone loves you for yourself alone!

NORAH *(colouring)* Sheilah!

SHEILAH *(quickly)* But you know, Aunt Girlie, what me and Norah do in our spare time is one of the most important jobs of the war.

GIRLIE Oh, what's that?

SHEILAH *(grinning wickedly)* Entertaining the troops! Our Tommies, the Yanks, the lot...

MUM At the YMCA. and the Red Cross, places like that.

SHEILAH In fact there's a dance tonight!

GIRLIE Tonight! But it's Sunday! You wouldn't go dancing on a Sunday, surely! Unless, of course, it's an officer's dance.

SHEILAH *(virtuously)* This dance is at an American Hospital Camp. Going there is like a...mercy mission.

GIRLIE Maggie, I'm surprised you'd let 'em go off with a bunch of foreigners like that. I wouldn't let my Sylvie go, I can assure you!

MUM Oh, men know a decent girl when they see one. I'm sure they'd never lay a hand on one of my girls!

SHEILAH Ivy, you are going to come, aren't you?

GIRLIE Maggie, surely not Ivy!

IVY Oh? Why not?

GIRLIE Oh...nothing...just thinking of poor Reg, I suppose...

IVY I think I will go, Mum. To keep Sheilah company.

MUM Yes, you go and have a good time.

IVY and SHEILAH exit.

NORAH *(calling after them)* I'm sorry I didn't get your skirt pressed, Sheilah.

SHEILAH *(poking her head back round door)* Anyone would think you were in love!

GIRLIE She's out of mourning then?

MUM I don't know if she's in or out, Girlie, and what's more, I don't care. All I know is Reg, God rest his soul, is dead, and Ivy's alive. I want to see her go dancing again — oh, don't look so shocked - instead of seeing her creeping round the house like a ghost! *(half-risen from her chair, leaning toward GIRLIE)* What's more, Girlie, since you're so interested, if she was to go dancing every night of the week, that'd be fine with me! There! And that's all I have to say in the matter! *(she subsides, pink in the face and breathless)*

GIRLIE Well...I never meant...I didn't mean anything...*(trailing off)*

MUM *(mollified)* That's all right then.

WARDEN *(offstage in a loud roar)* PUT THAT LIGHT OUT!

IVY *(from upstairs, offstage)* Sorry, Mr. Robbins!

MUM You girls! *(realizing NORAH is still there)* Aren't you going with your sisters?

NORAH Oh, not tonight.

GIRLIE And what will you be getting up to?

NORAH Oh, I have a date...

GIRLIE Oooh, Nooie...is it serious?

MUM What! Our Norah? Her middle name should have been fickle.

NORAH *(quickly as GIRLIE opens her mouth)* Aunt Girlie, what kind of fur is your coat?

MUM Norah, don't be personal.

GIRLIE No, no, that's all right, Maggie. That's all right. Well, it's not rabbit, Nooie, I can assure you of that! One of those old Conservatives tried to tell me it was Coney! I soon set him straight! "Coney?" I said. "Why, that's rabbit, and I wouldn't be seen dead wearing anything that common!" He didn't know what he was talking about! I've got it written right on the bill. Haven't I, Dinger? I made sure the furrier put it down. It's Lapin — L-A-P-I-N. It's an Australian mammal. That's what he said, Nooie. Rabbit indeed! This is Lapin!

NORAH *(startled)* Oh, it's very nice. Isn't it, Mum?

MUM Yes, very nice. *(beat)* Harry, can you tell me why we have so many sirens? They get me down more than the rationing even. We had four last night, didn't we? It seemed to be siren, all clear, siren, all clear, every five minutes. But no raid. I just don't understand it.

HARRY Well, you see—

GIRLIE Why, Maggie, no matter where those German bombers are headed for, they come in over the channel right above here. Imagine, right over us! Dinger says on a clear moonlight night you can count up to a hundred of 'em, all in formation.

MUM *(sighing)* This war, everybody's in the Front Line!

IVY and SHEILAH come clattering in, putting on their coats as they hurry to the back door.

IVY Cheerio, Mum.

They go to the door.

GIRLIE *(calling after them)* Don't forget now, "Keep your 'and on your 'a'penny". *(enjoying her vulgarity.)*

SHEILAH Got to rush, our ride's at six sharp.

They dash out.

GIRLIE Six? It's not six? Dinger, for heaven's sake, why didn't you say something? You know what those Conservatives are like! Have a fit, they would, if we weren't open in time for their evening tipple! Dinger! Get your coat!

NORAH *(jumping up)* I'll get it, Uncle Harry!

She goes to the hall and returns with his 'mac', which he puts on while the conversation continues.

GIRLIE Now when you're choosing among your boyfriends, Nooie, you be sure you do like my Sylvie. You catch yourself an officer.

NORAH looks upset at this.

HARRY Now, Girlie, the uniform doesn't make the man.

GIRLIE It makes for a much better marriage allowance, though, don't it?

MUM My girls have put aside any thoughts of marriage while this war is on. After what Ivy went through, they realize the foolishness of it. Now, Harry, dress up warm when you go out fire-watching, or next thing, you'll have pneumonia. *(getting up)* I'll see you to the door.

NORAH *(as GIRLIE and HARRY, followed by MUM, move to the door)* Cheerio, Auntie Girlie, Uncle Harry!

GIRLIE Good-bye Nooie. Come on, Dinger! Where's your torch!

HARRY Ta-ta, Nooie!

They exit to kitchen where we hear their last good-byes.

MUM *(offstage)* Mind the step!

NORAH has been standing at the table, half-heartedly piling up the dishes. She hears MUM coming back in, and we see her visibly straighten up, and paste a smile on her face.

MUM *(as she re-enters)* Now for a bit of peace and quiet! That Girlie, preening herself in that ridiculous coat.

NORAH Oh, Mum, didn't she! *(being as agreeable as she can)* And you know what, Mum? You know she said her coat was "Lapin"? Well, lapin's the French for rabbit!

MUM You don't say! I pity that furrier if she ever finds out!

NORAH That coat must have decimated the rabbit population, Mum!

MUM Yes. Oh, I'll be glad to put my feet up and have five minutes.

NORAH *(quickly)* I'll look after the dishes, Mum, but...well... I've got something real important I want to talk to you about, Mum.

MUM I just don't feel up to any more talk tonight.

NORAH Oh, but Mum...

MUM Be a good girl and get the table cleared off, and we'll talk tomorrow.

NORAH This is something special. Really it is!

MUM Now it's not a matter of life or death, is it? It can wait.

MUM goes over and collapses into her armchair, and closes her eyes. They remain closed for the rest of the scene.

NORAH Please, Mum, I must talk to you!

MUM *(her patience has run out.)* Not another word, or I won't even listen tomorrow — do you hear me?

NORAH *(close to tears)* Yes. I hear you.

She stands there dejected. Then she purposefully goes over to her handbag, takes out the consent form and goes determinedly back to MUM. She is just reaching down to touch her mother's arm to rouse her when a faint snore from MUM stops her. She looks from her mother to the paper, wavering. As she stands there, the stage slowly turns to black.

***

Act One, Scene Two

Three weeks later, Sunday morning.

MUM is sitting in her chair by the fire, reading the Sunday paper. IVY is sitting by the table, while SHEILAH styles her hair. NORAH is off-stage, in the kitchen, but we hear her moving around occasionally. While MUM is reading the paper she mutters disapprovingly, such things as, "Well, I never! etc.

SHEILAH Just sweep it up like this see...then make a sort of roll on top. The back's just a page-boy, turned under all round.

IVY Oh, I don't know.

SHEILAH You'll look just like Betty Grable! She wore her hair like this in "Moon Over Miami".

IVY Oh, I don't know...

SHEILAH Can't you say anything except "I don't know?" This uplift takes years off you!

IVY I didn't know I was looking so ancient!

SHEILAH Mum — don't you think our Ivy looks younger with her hair up like this? Mum! *(MUM is engrossed in the paper and doesn't answer.)* Oh, never mind! *(calling to kitchen)* Norah, come and tell us what you think of our Ivy's new hairstyle?

NORAH *(standing in the doorway)* What did you say? Oh, I like your hair like that, Ivy. It makes you look years younger!

IVY Thanks!

NORAH And more up-to-date...

IVY *(miffed)* I didn't realize I was so behind the times!

NORAH Well, now you can say you're "hep".

IVY Hep?

NORAH *(grinning)* Yeah, "in-the-swing"

SHEILAH *(to IVY)* Maybe...with your hair like this, you'll get "in the swing" tonight.

IVY Have you ever thought of opening a dating bureau?

SHEILAH The only man you showed any interest in was the one who couldn't ask you to dance. *(to NORAH)* He was on crutches.

IVY *(glancing over at MUM, who hasn't looked up, and whispering to SHEILAH)* I don't care whether I do or don't go to these dances — but if I don't go — which is likely if you don't stop pestering me — you can't go!

SHEILAH My lips are sealed.

IVY All right then.

SHEILAH *(picking up mirror and bobby-pins)* I'll go get changed.

She exits upstairs, stops and sniffs.

SHEILAH Is there something in the oven?

NORAH *(rushing off into the kitchen)* Ooh! My tarts!

IVY looks in the mirror, shakes her head "No" and puts her hair back to normal. She heads towards the stairs.

MUM *(looking up)* They're talking about cutting the cheese ration again.

IVY You can barely see it now. *(she exits upstairs)*

NORAH *(comes back in, carrying a pan of custard tarts fresh from the oven, and goes over to MUM)* Look, Mum, I made a dozen custard tarts. They turned out all right, didn't they?

MUM *(warily)* Yes, very nice.

NORAH I only used one egg, and not much milk. You'll have two left for the Yorkshire Pudding. *(no response)* That'll be a treat, won't it? I mean, it never comes up properly with that powdered stuff.

MUM Yes.

NORAH I just happened to be passing World Stores and it was just on the spur of the moment I went in. I thought Mr. Laing might have some biscuits for you, but no luck. Then he sort of whispered that he might have a cracked egg or two off the ration - and he came out with three! *(pausing, and looking at her mother appealingly)* Is there anything else I can do for you, Mum?

MUM I don't think so.

NORAH Are you sure? *(taking the consent form out of her pocket)*

MUM Yes, I'm sure! *(noticing the form, exasperated)* Look, my girl, you're wasting your time looking at me with those cow eyes. I don't intend to sign that consent form.

NORAH *(pleading)* But, Mum, Ben's done all the other paper work...

MUM But Mum, nothing. It's driving me to drink, you waving that blessed thing in my face. When are you going to give up?!

NORAH I'm not. I just can't! Mum, we found out yesterday, the Canadian Government has approved me.

MUM I should think they would.

NORAH Your consent is the only thing I need now.

MUM You're wasting your time!

NORAH Oh, if only I were six months older...I'd be twenty-one! I wouldn't need anyone's permission to get married.

MUM That's your attitude, is it? Well, my girl — that's what you'd best do then. Just wait until you're twenty-one! And leave me alone for good.

MUM is hurt and angry. She turns away from NORAH.

NORAH *(catching MUM by the arm)* Oh Mum, don't be like that! I don't want to go against you. I couldn't be happy if we had hard words, Mum. Getting married ought to be a happy time for everyone. What I was really meaning was that seeing as I can get married without permission when I'm twenty-one, why not say "Yes" now?

MUM I said "No" and that's final.

NORAH You don't care whether I'm happy or not, do you? You don't care if Ben gets moved away, and I never see him again. You'd be glad, wouldn't you?

She bursts into tears and runs, crying, upstairs, colliding with SHEILAH and IVY in the hall doorway.

SHEILAH What ever's the matter with our Norah, Mum?

MUM Need you ask! Morning, noon, and night for three whole weeks. That's all I've heard — "Please Mum, sign it! Please Mum, sign it!" — like a cracked gramophone record. I never thought she had it in her to be so headstrong! There's no talking sense to her anymore.

SHEILAH Never mind, Mum. She'll get over it.

MUM I hope you're right. What do you think, Ivy?

IVY Well...she does seem determined about this...

MUM Can't she see what trouble she's setting in store for herself? Even if she's lucky and he survives the war, she'll be going off to a strange place with a man she scarcely knows. How does she know he's not telling her a pack of lies like that one with Girlie's butcher's niece? If I say yes, and something went wrong over there she wouldn't have a soul to turn to.

IVY Mum, try not to upset yourself.

MUM I hoped we were going to have a nice quiet Sunday today for a change.

She sighs, and picks up the paper, but throws it down again in disgust.

MUM Well, nothing to cheer you up in the paper. Now there's this daylight bombing...

SHEILAH Charlie told me we're losing all sorts of planes.

MUM Who's Charlie?

SHEILAH Just a friend. You know me, Mum. I'm not the marrying kind. Not for ages, anyway.

MUM That's good.

SHEILAH Ivy's coming to the dance with me again tonight, Mum.

MUM How's that jitter-bug business coming on then, Ivy?

IVY Well, I'm not as good as Sheilah yet.

MUM Oh, you soon will be.

SHEILAH Mum, why don't you go up and have a bit of a rest. That meat will cook itself more or less, won't it?

MUM I don't know when I've seen a more pathetic piece of meat, and it's our whole week's ration. If it's to do us for three days, we'll need a miracle like the loaves and fishes.

SHEILAH Ivy'll keep an eye on it, see it doesn't get too dry, won't you, Ivy?

IVY *(surprised)* Where will you be then? You going out?

SHEILAH *(quickly)* Yes, didn't I tell you? I thought I did. You see, Mum, Jean Oliver's making me a dress and I was supposed to take the material and pattern over to her yesterday, but I forgot, so I'd better get it over to her today. She's hard up and needs the money.

MUM But she lives right down town, doesn't she? What about your dinner? You'll never be able to get back by dinner time...

SHEILAH Mmm...the way the buses are on a Sunday...you're probably right. Well, I'll just have to go without, won't I? Perhaps I can get a bite with her, or at the pub. I could take her out for a treat. Since she had the baby, and with her husband in the Middle East, she doesn't get out much.

MUM I don't like you missing your Sunday dinner.

SHEILAH Neither do I. Still, never mind. Oh! And if she takes too long doing all the measuring up — she does fuss so - I may have to settle for meeting Ivy where we pick up the truck for the dance, - you never know...

MUM *(doubtfully)* Well, I'll save your dinner anyway. But you will try to get home, won't you?

SHEILAH Thanks, Mum. Of course I will, Mum.

MUM Well then, I'll go on up. But Ivy, wake me up at two o'clock.

IVY Yes. Have a good rest.

IVY is staring hard at SHEILAH. As soon as MUM is safely out of the way upstairs, she wheels round on SHEILAH.

That was the biggest load of codswallop I've heard in a long time! Just what are you up to?

SHEILAH Nothing for you to get excited about.

IVY Then why all the lies? We both know that Jean Oliver moved down to Devon last year to live with her mother-in-law.

SHEILAH Yes, well — as long as Mum doesn't know, it's all right, isn't it?

IVY Come on. What's this about?

SHEILAH It's called an alibi. I'm going up to London for the night — with Charlie.

IVY You're what?

SHEILAH You heard me.

IVY This is a joke, isn't it? You're pulling my leg.

SHEILAH No. I'm going - right now, as a matter of fact, or we'll miss the train.

IVY I thought you had more sense than to pull a stunt like this!

SHEILAH So did I. But you know what they say — "due to circumstances beyond my control..."

IVY *(shocked)* Don't be so damned flippant! And what about Mum? How can you do this to her!

SHEILAH I've got it all worked out! With your help, Mum'll be none the wiser.

IVY What!!

SHEILAH It's quite simple. I've covered myself as far as the dance, haven't I? Well, Mum's always snoring away when we get back, so I've just got to show up at breakfast. The paper train from London gets in to Bournemouth at 5:30 a.m., and as long as I'm on it, there'll be no problem. I'll just slip quietly in the front door, straight up the stairs, into bed, and get up at seven as usual. The only thing I'm asking you to do is make sure the front door is unlocked.

IVY You're not roping me in on this. No.

SHEILAH Look, I didn't expect you to want to do it for me, but I thought you'd do it for Mum's sake.

There's a pause while IVY wrestles with this.

IVY *(unhappy)* All right. For Mum's sake.

SHEILAH Thanks, then I'm off.

She goes to the hall and returns with hat, coat, and small bag.

Ta ta for now! (*picking up her purse*)

IVY But what about the dance? Do you expect me to go on my own?

SHEILAH Say you're getting the 'flu. Or pretend you missed the truck.

IVY (*as SHEILAH heads for the door*) Sheilah!

SHEILAH *(turning back to IVY)* I've got good reasons.

SHEILAH exits. IVY stands, staring after her.

IVY Damn! Oh, damn!

NORAH comes from upstairs, looking unhappy.

NORAH Was that the door?

IVY It's not "your Ben". Don't bother to come down.

NORAH There's no need to snap at me!

IVY I'll snap at you if I feel like it. And I feel like it!

NORAH What have I done?

IVY Done? You and Sheilah...you're a fine pair. All you think of is yourselves. You care nothing for Mum.

NORAH That's not fair!

IVY You decide you want to get married, so what does it matter that you're making her life miserable.

NORAH If anyone's being made miserable, it's me! Why can't you see my side of it for a change?

IVY You know it's bad for her to get upset. You know her heart's worn out — all those years she spent piece work ironing in that damned laundry.

NORAH But why are you throwing that up to me?

IVY She was doing it for you...for all us kids...to put bread on the table, because your father walked out on her.

NORAH Because my father walked out? That's my fault too?

IVY No, but you aren't making life easier for her, are you?

NORAH I don't need a lecture from you. I know the sacrifices she made. Look, I just want to get married. What has that got to do with what happened twenty years ago?

IVY It has everything to do with it. You could wind up exactly like she did.

NORAH You mean you think Ben would desert me like my father did her? Oh, that's ridiculous.

IVY It's wartime. Anything can happen. Do you think Mum thought her marriage to your father would end like it did? And before that...do you think she thought

IVY *(continued)* my father's ship would go down? Anymore than I thought Reg's would? What's tearing Mum apart is that you're making the same mistake she did. *(pause)* And that I did. Oh, Norah, she tried to warn me, you know...when war broke out...but I wouldn't listen. I was just the way you are...I thought it couldn't happen to me. But it did.

NORAH Oh, Ivy...I understand what you've been through.

IVY You understand what I've been through? How could you. People are always making these glib remarks. "I understand!" How can they know what it was like ...trying to sort out all the rumours that were going around when the *Firedrake* was sunk? The Admiralty never wanted to admit that one of our ships had gone down. They waited weeks, sometimes months, before they let the families know. The only thing we could do was listen to those nightly broadcasts from Germany. That traitor, Lord Haw Haw — he was always the first one to name the ships their U Boats had sunk. So you sat and listened to him gloating about the glorious Third Reich, and jeering at the British people for letting that war-mongering Winston Churchill lead us into a hopeless war. We listened, just hoping for a few scraps of information.

NORAH Oh, Ivy.

IVY And do you really think you "understand" how it felt to pick up the newspaper one morning, and see a picture of a life-raft from the *Firedrake* — a life raft that had been floating around in the Pacific for weeks with the bodies of dead sailors aboard — and to wonder if one of them was your husband? I don't think so.

NORAH Mum hid that paper. We didn't think you saw it.

IVY Oh, I saw it all right — at work. By the time the Admiralty finally admitted the *Firedrake* had been sunk, and sent me their usual "The Admiralty regrets" telegram, it was stale news...

They both sit silent for a while.

IVY Mum doesn't want to see you hurt. Neither do I.

NORAH I know.

IVY Please, Norah, think about the consequences. Ask yourself if you really want to spend every day and every night wondering if your husband is alive or dead?

Suddenly, a bomb whistles down. Then another, closer. NORAH gets up. They look at each other in horror, momentarily. The Air Raid Siren sounds the Alert, which galvanizes them into action. IVY shouts, "Mum." and heads up the stairs, NORAH on her heels, but at the doorway IVY stops her.

IVY I'll get Mum. You go and get under the table-shelter. Norah! Go on! Move!

NORAH nods, and rushes to the front room. The noise outside is escalating. We hear a plane, men's voices yelling, and a piercing whistle blown, glass breaking. More bombs are whistling down. All the sounds of pandemonium one would expect, as IVY goes upstairs calling MUM.

Blackout.

***

Act Two, Scene One

About an hour later, after the air-raid.

We hear the sound of perhaps two Spitfires, at first overhead, but then trailing away, a heavy vehicle, men's voices, then the siren sounding the "All Clear". On stage, we find one picture hanging crooked on the wall, and two on the floor. A piece of the ornamental plaster around the ceiling is on the floor, but that seems to be the extent of the damage.

MUM, NORAH, and IVY emerge, cautiously looking around, from the front room.

MUM Our Sheilah could be buried under a pile of rubble for all we know.

NORAH Mum, they've got air-raid shelters fixed up under all the big stores, you know they have.

IVY Where's your medicine, Mum? In the kitchen?

MUM Next to the tea caddy. Thanks, Ivy.

NORAH *(looking around)* I'm surprised this window's still in one piece.

IVY *(off)* All the years we've bitched about that Morrison table-shelter, but I was grateful for that steel plate over me when I heard those bombs.

NORAH I thought the house was going to come down round us a couple of times. *(picking up a picture)* Oh, Ivy, the glass is broken in your father's picture.

MUM Norah, you don't suppose Sheilah's phoned next door? Go round and ask Mrs. Sutton?

NORAH I doubt if the phones are working, Mum.

IVY *(re-entering with pills and water)* The lines will be tied up anyway. Mum, you need to get that prescription renewed, you know. You're down to a couple of pills.

NORAH I'm sure she'll telephone when she can, and Mrs. Sutton will let us know. But don't worry, Mum, she really was safer downtown than we were.

MUM But that's where all the bombs were falling! Oh, why did she have to go to the dress maker's today of all days.

IVY I'm going to look upstairs...see if there's any damage.

NORAH Mum, I bet you'd like a cup of tea, eh? I'll put the kettle on, shall I?

MUM All right. *(as NORAH starts for the kitchen.)* Oh, no! We'd better not, Norah. It might not be safe to light the gas.

NORAH *(suddenly)* Look, there's Mr. Robbins, just over the road.

MUM He should know about down town...

MUM hurries out the back door, and we hear her calling off-stage.

MUM Mr. Robbins! Mr. Robbins!

IVY *(off)* Both the back bedroom windows are cracked.

NORAH Ivy, she's too worried about Sheilah to care about windows.

IVY Oh God, what a mess.

NORAH Sheilah might have been hurt, you know. It did sound like the bombs were down town.

IVY The bombs may have been, but Sheilah wasn't.

NORAH What do you mean?

IVY You weren't in on it?

NORAH In on what?

IVY Norah, our little sister is on a train to London — to spend the night with her precious flyer.

NORAH Charlie? I don't believe you.

IVY She told me straight out that was what she was going to do.

NORAH Oh, Ivy...what if she gets pregnant!

IVY We can't worry about that. We've got to figure out what we're going to say to Mum. Sheilah thought she could sneak in before morning, but that won't work now. Mum's just going to sit here all day waiting for Sheilah. And Sheilah won't be home until tomorrow morning.

NORAH Oh...but we can't let her fret all night long.

We hear the gate click and see MUM coming back in.

IVY *(tidying something in the room)* For now, try to act normal.

NORAH All right. *(starts tidying up)*

MUM comes in looking worried.

MUM You were right about the phone lines...and the trolley buses aren't running. So...we can't expect Sheilah for a while.

IVY I'm sure she's fine, Mum. You know what you're always telling us, don't meet trouble half way.

MUM That's right. Norah...you can go and make that cup of tea. Mr. Robbins says it's all right to use the gas-stove. *(as soon as NORAH has cleared)* Ivy...*(beckoning IVY over to her)*

IVY What is it, Mum?

MUM Shhh...*(after NORAH is out of hearing, beckoning to IVY to come close)* Ivy, do you know where Ben's billet was?

IVY *(surprised)* Norah's Ben?

MUM Of course Norah's Ben! Where was his billet?

IVY I don't know...why?

MUM Mr. Robbins says that he heard that there was a direct hit on one of the Canadian billets.

IVY Oh, my God. Where was it? She told me once.

MUM He wasn't sure which...but the way he talked things look pretty black.

IVY Oh, poor Norah.

MUM Well, we don't know for sure...and like we just said, there's no sense in meeting trouble half way.

We see HARRY and GIRLIE pass the window.

IVY Oh, no...

MUM Oh, please God, not today...

We hear them coming in to the kitchen.

GIRLIE *(off, to NORAH)* Nooie, you're all right?

MUM Not a word of anything in front of Girlie, Ivy!

HARRY and GIRLIE enter.

GIRLIE Well, Maggie! We come straight over, didn't wait for the 'All Clear'. I said to Dinger, didn't I, Dinger, I can't sit comfortable until I know that poor Maggie's not blown into Kingdom Come by one of those bombs!

MUM Well, thanks, Girlie.

HARRY Are you feeling all right, Maggie?

MUM A bit shook up, that's all. Oh, Harry, I'm glad to see you.

IVY We got off light, thank goodness, Uncle Harry — no damage to speak of.

NORAH enters with tea tray.

GIRLIE There's a lot of damage downtown. A lot! It's a mess, isn't it, Dinger, the big stores, Bobby's, Beale's, the West Cinema, Trinity Church...

MUM Was anybody hurt?

HARRY We didn't hear of any civilian casualties...

GIRLIE Yes, Dinger, but those poor Canadian soldiers ...eating their lunch they were. Direct hit! Killed instantly, everyone of them!

NORAH, in the act of bringing tea, drops the tray with a crash, and stands there unheeding. All eyes are on her.

MUM Norah, don't go thinking the worst!

GIRLIE What's the matter?

IVY We don't know that it's Ben's billet.

IVY mops up the floor.

GIRLIE Who's Ben? *(as IVY shakes her head at GIRLIE)* What's going on? Did I speak out of turn?

HARRY Nooie...is one of these Canadians your young man, then?

NORAH just nods, too overcome to speak.

Now, look, Nooie...like your Mum said don't go thinking the worst. We don't even know for certain it was soldiers. It's true that a bomb fell on one of the Canadian billets, but some say it was airmen there.

MUM Norah, come on. Listen to your uncle.

NORAH I'm sorry...I'm sorry *...(unable to finish and turning away, trying to control herself)*

GIRLIE Well, Maggie. It's too bad you hadn't told me she had a Canadian boyfriend...or you know me, I'd never have said a word.

HARRY Maggie, Girlie and I will be on our way now.

MUM *(her eyes on NORAH)* Yes...thank you, Harry...

GIRLIE In a minute, Dinger.

HARRY Girlie...

GIRLIE This Canadian — it looks like it's serious then...

HARRY Girlie...

GIRLIE ...or was, at any rate.

HARRY I can't remember whether I locked the back door...

GIRLIE Dinger, how could you be so careless! We could be robbed blind. Sorry, Maggie, but...*(on her way out)*

MUM I understand. Goodbye. *(quietly)* Harry, thank you.

HARRY and GIRLIE exit. MUM turns toward NORAH.

IVY *(after a beat)* Is there anything I can do?

MUM *(shaking her head)* No, no, you go on.

IVY Well, then, I'll go on up to the surgery, and get your prescription refilled.

MUM Drop in and have a word with Mrs. Robbins on the way back. See if there's any more news.

IVY exits. Silence between MUM and NORAH.

MUM Now, Norah, I'm sure someone would let you know if...anything had happened to Ben.

NORAH I'm just a girlfriend, aren't I? Girlfriends don't count. Who would bother to tell me anything?

Silence.

MUM Norah, listen to me...

NORAH Mum, I don't feel like talking about it.

Silence.

MUM Please, don't shut me out.

NORAH What is there to say?

MUM Perhaps it's me that needs to talk, Norah. I can feel every day how you resent me not signing that paper, and it hurts that you think I'm against you.

NORAH I know you aren't making me miserable on purpose.

MUM I'm trying to protect you.

NORAH But you can't...not from everything in my life. You have to let me make my own decisions...

MUM But you're still so young.

NORAH I'm an adult. I've been bringing you home my wages since I was fourteen. I've done my share to keep us going.

MUM I know that, you and Ivy and Sheilah, I know how much I owe you.

NORAH I'm not looking for thanks, Mum. I can never repay you for all the years you worked so hard for us. That's not what I'm trying to say. I'm trying to make you see that I think it's wrong of you to treat me like a child. It's time you stopped that.

MUM But this marriage, you're asking me to go against my conscience.

NORAH Because you think Ben is somehow like my father...but I wouldn't want to marry a man who was so despicable.

MUM Despicable! How did you get the idea he was despicable? I've never said any such thing.

NORAH No, you've never said anything at all. He was a forbidden subject in this house.

MUM There's some things I thought it was better you don't know, that's all.

NORAH There you go protecting me again. But how do you think I feel when Aunt Girlie goes on about that good-for-nothing who deserted us?

MUM You know better than to mind Girlie...

NORAH And why did you tell us he was dead? Why did you let me go to school on Armistice Day wearing a poppy to show my father was killed in the war the same as Madge and Ivy's was?

MUM When you were a little girl, you mean? But it was you that wanted to wear it. You wanted to stand up on the platform with your sisters...and I didn't have the heart to tell you you shouldn't.

NORAH I wish you had. One Armistice Day...when I was nine years old, Beryl Haines came up to me after the ceremony and yelled at me I had no right to be there. Because my father hadn't been killed at all. He'd just run off and left us.

MUM Oh, Norah...

NORAH I didn't believe her..."Don't be so daft," she said. "My Mum says you weren't even born till five years after the war was over." I called her a liar, and then ran all the way home. I can still remember how she laughed.

MUM I couldn't find the right words to tell you...I should have tried...somehow.

NORAH I should have figured it out myself. I knew how to add by then. It just never crossed my mind that you could lie to me.

MUM But I never knew you had any trouble? Why didn't you come to me?

NORAH I asked Ivy, that day when I got home from school, and she said don't ever mention your father to Mum... not ever...she made me swear it. So I never did. But I started to hate him...I started to worry that I had bad blood in me and that I'd turn out to be no good just like him.

MUM I thought I was smoothing out an awkward situation, but...I couldn't tell you about your father, it was too difficult. You see, when he married me...he committed bigamy.

NORAH Mum!

MUM I didn't know it — but he already had a wife and children in Ireland. There...I've never told that to a living soul. Even your Uncle Harry doesn't know.

NORAH Oh...

MUM But it wasn't his fault, Norah, not really.

NORAH Not his fault!

MUM No, now you listen. He was a good man.

NORAH looks like she might protest again.

Yes, a good man. When we met he'd just been invalided out of the army, he was sick, lonely, confused, and in a strange country. I was a war widow struggling to bring up Madge and Ivy on my own. It was a case of two lonely people...six weeks later we were married. Oh, it sounds like I did a foolish thing, but...if you had known him. He could charm the birds off the trees if he'd a mind to.

NORAH He lied to you...he deceived you!

MUM Yes, he did. Because he wanted to be with me. Because he loved me. Don't judge him, Norah. He was a good man who made one mistake. He was impulsive just like you are.

NORAH Me?

MUM Oh, Norah, you're so like him...you've got so many of his ways. You think with your hands, the same way he did. He was a skilled carpenter and cabinet maker, and he could draw and paint and carve things.

NORAH How else am I like him?

MUM You have his eyes. You walk like him. You lift your shoulder and shrug just like he did.

NORAH I still don't know why he left us.

MUM Well...his conscience nagged at him twenty-four hours a day. That's what he told me. One night, after he'd had a good drink — he'd started to drink when he couldn't hold a job — his lungs were giving him so much trouble. He'd been gassed at the Somme, you see. He was so depressed, poor man, he got that he couldn't live with himself anymore — so he poured out the whole story to me. He didn't know what to do. He was so unhappy. My heart ached for him. I knew the right thing for him to do was to go back to his wife. He didn't just run off and leave us. It was plain to see that he hated to go. I don't know if you can understand this, Norah, but...well, Ivy's father was a decent man...marrying him was the sensible thing to do...but with your father it was different...I loved him the moment I laid eyes on him. I knew he was the only man I ever could love.

NORAH I do understand, Mum. Because that's the way I feel about Ben.

Fade to black.

***

Act Two, Scene Two

The next morning, around 9:30.

IVY and MUM are sitting over tea and toast. IVY is in her housecoat. They are listening to the radio. The text of the news broadcast used in the Blyth Festival production is found in production notes at the front of the book.

IVY That toast's cold, Mum. Shall I make you a fresh piece?

MUM No, I don't think so. Perhaps later on I'll feel more like it.

IVY All right.

MUM When do you have to go to work?

IVY Not 'til three o'clock. *(turning off the radio)* The priority is shifted to landing craft...all the Admiralty stuff.

MUM Then I guess the invasion really will be this summer.

IVY Early summer, if the rumours are right.

MUM That's not very far away, is it? *(pause)* Is Norah awake yet?

IVY I heard her moving around a while ago.

MUM She was up most of the night, Ivy. She shouldn't go into work.

IVY I'll run round to Mrs. Sutton's and ring her boss, shall I?

MUM In your housecoat?

IVY It's only next door.

IVY might put something on over her housecoat or just tie it more securely. They hear the latch gate click and IVY looks towards the window.

IVY *(not certain how MUM will react)* It's Sheilah, Mum.

MUM Oh.

MUM starts up and heads to the door. Then she stops and goes back to her chair and sits down again. SHEILAH comes in and looks at her mother, then at IVY, then back at her mother. She can see from IVY that her mother knows all. IVY exits.

MUM So, you've come home, have you?

SHEILAH Yes, Mum. Mum...I...

MUM You must be proud of yourself. Oh, yes. I know all about it. Ivy told me last night.

SHEILAH I'm sorry, Mum. Really I am...but Charlie and me...

MUM *(cutting her off)* I don't think I want to hear any more than I know already. I'm disappointed in you, Sheilah — I've always trusted you girls. I've always been able to say that my girls would never let me down. You've been my pride and joy.

SHEILAH I never meant to hurt you. I never meant to hurt anybody. Oh, Mum, I've made such a mess of everything. I've been such a fool.

MUM No, Sheilah. I was the fool. The fool who was taken in by all your lies. The fool who was worrying because you'd miss your Sunday dinner. The fool who spent half the night worrying whether you were buried under the rubble of some bombed building.

NORAH comes down.

MUM *(motioning to NORAH to her own chair)* Norah, sit here. *(pouring her a cup of tea)* I'm going to make you some toast with real butter on it. *(handing her the tea)*

NORAH I don't want anything, Mum.

MUM I'm going to make it and you're going to eat it, and that's that.

NORAH All right, Mum...when I've drunk my tea.

SHEILAH Mum, there's something I need to tell you.

MUM I don't want to know. I'm concerned with Norah's worries right now.

IVY *(entering)* Your boss says you can take the day off, Norah.

SHEILAH Why? What's wrong?

IVY *(aside to SHEILAH)* There was a direct hit on a Canadian billet...It may have been Ben's.

SHEILAH Oh, no, is that what you think? No, it's not true. Really it's not. Norah, believe me. It was Canadians, but it was airmen — a sergeant's mess. Nowhere near Ben at all.

NORAH You're sure? You're really sure?

SHEILAH I was talking to a Canadian airman at the station. Yes, I'm really sure.

NORAH *(laughing and crying)* Oh, Sheilah. Thank you, thank you. Oh, Mum.

NORAH runs over and hugs all three in turn, MUM, NORAH and IVY are laughing and crying.

MUM Just look at us. What are we crying for?

NORAH I can't help it. I'm just so happy...

SHEILAH Mum, listen...

MUM No, the less I know about it the better.

The gate latch clicks. HARRY passes the window. IVY sees him.

IVY Mum, it's Uncle Harry...

MUM Just Harry, not Girlie?

IVY I didn't see her. *(as MUM exits)* And she'd be hard to miss.

MUM *(off)* Well, Harry...this is a surprise...

HARRY *(off)* I just stopped by for a minute...*(as they come on)* You heard Ben's lot were all right?

MUM Yes, thank God. *(HARRY stands dejectedly)* Is something wrong? *(HARRY hesitates.)* Girlie's not sick, is she? *(HARRY shakes his head)* Harry, there's something on your mind, isn't there? Come and sit down, or we could go in the front room if you'd prefer to have some privacy?

HARRY No, the girls ought to hear what I've got to say. It won't be a secret much longer anyway. *(pauses)* It's our Sylvie, Maggie. *(blurting it out)* She's in the family way.

Silence.

MUM Oh, Harry, I'm so sorry.

HARRY *(pause)* I know she's not the first and she won't be the last. But that's not much comfort when it's your own. She's not a bad girl, Maggie.

MUM Well, of course she isn't. Bad girls don't have babies because they're too fly to get caught. It's the good girls because they're innocent...they just don't know anything. *(to the girls)* Why don't you girls go and get some clothes on?

They exit.

HARRY Girlie had her suspicions...but Sylvie denied it over and over again...swore she couldn't be. I don't understand...why wouldn't she tell us?

MUM It sounds like the poor girl was just plain frightened. Girlie wouldn't be easy on her.

HARRY No, not easy. What she called Sylvie! Oh, I know Sylvie done wrong, but Girlie...she didn't need to be so hard on her.

MUM What about the father, Harry? One of those officers?

HARRY An officer! You know how Girlie exaggerates. No, the boy is just an ordinary seaman. Not that I think any the worse of him for that. Only nineteen. Same age as Sylvie. Arthur's his name. Arthur Pitts.

MUM Will they get married, do you think? Or haven't they decided yet?

HARRY They didn't get the chance, Maggie. Girlie did all the deciding. They were married on Friday by special licence at the registry office.

MUM That was quick.

HARRY I wanted to tell you myself before some busy body made it their business to.

MUM What's the boy like then?

HARRY He's a local lad, fond of Sylvie. I think he had it in mind to marry her before, but in Girlie's eyes he wasn't good enough. He's in the Merchant Navy on those Russian convoys. He'll be off again as soon as his ship's repaired. I wish I was going with him.

MUM Some days, I'd join you, Harry.

HARRY You, Maggie? But your girls have never been much trouble?

MUM My girls are no different than any others. When I'm not worrying about Ivy, sitting around like she's waiting for the world to end, and Sheilah, thinking of nothing but a good time, I've always got Norah, and between you and me, Harry, she's been leading me a fine old dance. Head over heels in love with this Canadian soldier, who could be the next Jack the Ripper for all we know.

HARRY Oh, I doubt that.

MUM They don't realize what a worry they are. Or they don't care.

HARRY Did you, Maggie, when you married Pat McKernan? I well remember how worried our Dad was. *(MUM looks at him)* And you could hardly blame him. It wasn't just that you'd known him only a few weeks, he knew you'd lose your navy pension when you remarried.

MUM I can see how he must have felt...of course, it didn't look like that to me. I was so headstrong.

HARRY And then you went and spent your last couple of shillings on that fancy mirror instead of the saucepan you set out to buy. That was the last straw. He was really disgusted with you then.

MUM What mirror?

HARRY You must remember! "Well, Meggist," he said, "Now thee can zit theeself down in front of thick looking glass and watch theeself starve to death."

MUM Oh. Harry, I was an awful fool, wasn't I? And to think that I — *(she stops suddenly)*

HARRY *(knowing where her thoughts have gone)* It's all a part of being young, Maggie. We had to make our own mistakes.

MUM slowly nods her head.

But look at it this way, Maggie. On paper it may look like the stupidest damn fool thing anyone could ever do, but it got you your Nooie and Sheilah, didn't it? So perhaps you weren't such a fool after all.

MUM *(a moment between them)* Thank you, Harry. Thank you.

HARRY *(rousing himself)* Girlie was such a pretty little thing when I married her, you know. That's why they called her Girlie.

MUM Sylvie looks a lot like her.

HARRY *(beat)* I shouldn't have let Girlie have all the say in bringing up the girls. There were times I should have put my foot down.

MUM You've done your best, Harry.

HARRY Mother used to say "We plan, and God unplans."

MUM She had a saying for every situation. I hear myself repeating them to my girls, and they grin behind my back just like we did behind hers.

HARRY She was a wise woman — even though I don't think she was ever five miles from home.

MUM The first war changed our lives a lot, didn't it?

HARRY nods.

This one's going to change things even more.

HARRY And you might as well try to empty the ocean with a teacup...

MUM *(joining in)*...as try to stop it.

HARRY and MUM share a smile.

HARRY Well, I must be getting back. Still got the bar to open. *(calling up stairs)* Good-bye, girls. Glad your young man's all right, Nooie. *(to MUM)* Don't get up. I'll see myself out.

HARRY exits. SHEILAH comes down.

SHEILAH Mum...

MUM looks at her.

SHEILAH Mum, I've got to talk to you.

MUM Go on, then.

SHEILAH I know I told you me and Charlie were just friends, Mum. In a way it was true, but we like each other a lot, and if there wasn't a war on we'd probably be thinking of getting engaged...me deciding to go up to London with him — well, it wasn't something just for fun. He'd been having a lot of trouble with his nerves. Two of his best friends were shot down last week and he got so depressed...and he said he really needed me. I felt it was the right thing to do...going I mean. But at the hotel...he wanted me to marry him right away, and I was afraid, I don't really understand why, and said I'd just been stringing him along...and we had an argument...and I got mad, walked out, and spent the night in a tube station.

MUM I see.

SHEILAH I've got to say it, Mum. I think I should have stayed with him. I was stupid to be afraid. I let him down. Do you understand, Mum?

MUM Well...*(one woman to another)* this war's like the last one — nothing's just black or white, is it?

MUM gets up and heads upstairs and meets NORAH coming down.

NORAH Going to have a rest, Mum?

MUM No, no. There's something I want to take a look for, that's all.

NORAH *(to SHEILAH)* Well...did she listen?

SHEILAH *(nods)* I think she's forgiven me. I just wish Charlie would.

NORAH If you went to see him...maybe you could explain...

SHEILAH If he'd hadn't sprung it on me...if he hadn't demanded that I marry him on the spot. All I could think of was the good times I'd miss out on, being able to do whatever I wanted...going to the dances...

NORAH Once I met Ben I lost interest in that kind of thing.

SHEILAH I thought you were such an idiot. Now I'm not so sure...

NORAH I was an idiot. All that kid stuff about my wedding day.

SHEILAH Norah!

NORAH Oh, I still want to get married...but just to be with Ben...to have a life together...for however long or short it is...I want to be his wife.

IVY enters in her work clothes.

SHEILAH I was so clever to calculate Charlie's odds for survival. I could have been trying to make him happy, like Ivy did for Reg. I still remember -- oh, I'm sorry, Ivy...

IVY What do you remember?

SHEILAH The day he left to go back to his ship. What he said to you...about how happy you'd made him...and how he looked at you...that's all.

IVY stares at her for a moment, then turns away. A moment. MUM comes downstairs, humming to herself, with a mirror with a tarnished silver frame. They look at her, astonished.

MUM I thought I'd give this old mirror a shine. It always came up lovely.

SHEILAH I don't remember seeing that...

MUM Oh, it's been in my bottom drawer for years...*(exiting into the kitchen)* Why don't you see if there's something on the wireless?

SHEILAH *(going to the wireless and finding jitter-bug music)* Come on, Norah.

NORAH No, you and Ivy go ahead.

NORAH goes to her handbag on the sideboard and takes out the consent form and puts it in her pocket.

SHEILAH Ive?

IVY At ten o'clock in the morning?

SHEILAH Why not?

IVY Right, why not?

MUM comes back with silver polish and a cloth in time to see IVY and SHEILAH dancing. She sits and polishes the mirror, smiling. NORAH watches her. Then she comes to a decision, goes over and turns the radio off.

IVY Norah!

NORAH Just for a minute. I want to talk to Mum. *(going to her)* Mum, you told me I'd be sorry if I married Ben while the war was still on. Well, last night I didn't know if he'd been killed or not...and it was horrible. But I really think...I am sure, Mum, not being married to him doesn't help...in fact, it's worse. If Ben and I were married...if I was his wife...I 'd feel part of him. So, Mum, I have the consent form here...Please Mum, sign it.

MUM *(looks at her for a moment)* I've been thinking about it too, Norah. Your Uncle Harry reminded me of some things...well, no need to go into that. At any rate — if you make your bed, you'll have to lie in it, so you have the right to make your own decision. *(NORAH is astonished, so are the other girls)* Well, don't just stand there. Give me the paper before I start to remember how far away Canada is! And a pen!

There's a general flap.

IVY *(finding one)* Here.

MUM *(signing with a flourish)* There you are, for better or worse.

NORAH *(taking it)* Oh, Mum.

SHEILAH slips out of the room quietly.

MUM I suppose you'd better bring that Ben of yours in to see me if he's to be one of the family.

NORAH Oh, yes, Mum, I will.

MUM I'm afraid I can't quite call him to mind, Norah. There have been so many...

NORAH Well, he's dark and he's got greyish greenish eyes...

MUM I don't know if I've taken much note of all these young men's eyes.

NORAH Oh. *(idea)* Oh, he brought you a big tin of corned beef.

MUM Now I remember him. He apologised that it was only corned beef. Well, well, so that was Ben.

SHEILAH returns with a brown paper parcel which she puts into NORAH's arms.

SHEILAH Here! Here's your first wedding present!

They all crowd around as NORAH opens it. She pulls out a handful of white silk.

NORAH *(blankly)* It's a parachute?

SHEILAH No, you dope. It's your wedding dress. *(NORAH is still blank)* There's yards and yards of white silk there...so you'd better get busy.

IVY has been reading the consent form, she holds it out to MUM.

IVY Mum, this has to be dated too.

SHEILAH March the fifth.

MUM takes the form and writes in the date.

NORAH April, May...June the fifth...June 5th, 1944 — that will be my wedding day, Mum. June fifth.

Fade to black.

***

Act Two, Scene Three

Sunday afternoon, June 4, 1944. IVY and SHEILAH are ironing skirts, blouses, hat veils. IVY has a new stylish hair do. GIRLIE and HARRY and MUM are sitting at the table, tea things in evidence.

GIRLIE And if I haven't had enough to put up with, can you believe this, Maggie, some sneak thief has broken into the drinks cupboard at the club!

MUM Really?

GIRLIE Dinger didn't notice, did you, Dinger? But I keep track of the stock. There was a bottle of gin, a bottle of scotch, and two bottles of sherry — just disappeared overnight. I got my suspicions who the thief is. It would have to be a member. And for my money, it's that beady-eyed blighter who tried to tell me my coat was rabbit.

HARRY You shouldn't say that. You've no proof.

GIRLIE Oh, Dinger thinks everyone's as honest as he is, but those bottles didn't sprout legs and run off on their own, did they? *(sips her tea and grimaces)* I know there's a war on, Maggie, but this is cricket's piddle today for sure.

NORAH comes in from the kitchen with MUM'S best pair of shoes. She holds them up for MUM'S approval.

MUM It's not the war, it's the wedding. Norah, without even a by-your-leave, swapped my Typhoo Tips for the coupons for her going-away outfit. *(as HARRY takes the last bit of plum jam)* Enjoy that last bit of jam, Harry, because she traded the sugar I'd been hoarding as well.

NORAH Oh, Mum...I had to have icing sugar for my cake.

SHEILAH At least when she's married off, our rations will be safe.

NORAH exits upstairs with the shoes. SHEILAH follows with the clothes as IVY moves ironing board back to kitchen.

HARRY You've got to give your Nooie credit, Maggie, she hasn't missed a trick, has she?

MUM It's the bridegroom who may be missed, Harry.

GIRLIE What? You mean the wedding's going to be off?

MUM She hasn't heard from Ben for weeks.

GIRLIE You can't trust any of those chaps from overseas! They're only after one thing and they'll promise a girl anything to get it! Even marriage. But when it's time to walk down the aisle, they get cold feet.

MUM It's not like that at all, Girlie. His company's behind barbed wire. Forbidden to leave camp. Ben sneaked out and phoned her once so she'd understand how things were.

HARRY He'd have been up on charges if they'd caught him.

MUM Norah's sure he'll turn up. Hoped he'd be here lunch time. Even wangled a pork chop out of the butcher for him. Now it's after tea, and still no sign of him.

HARRY If they're behind barbed wire, there's only one reason. It's the invasion, Maggie.

GIRLIE That'll be that, then. The wedding's off for sure.

MUM Girlie, don't go saying that to Norah, not yet.

HARRY No, it's not—

GIRLIE If you ask me, it's a blessing in disguise. You don't want your Nooie to go off to that outlandish place, and live in a log hut — with all that ice and snow and blizzards all year round.

MUM Rubbish, Girlie. *(crossing to stairs and calling to NORAH)* Norah...where's that calendar?

GIRLIE And with Red Indians waitin' to scalp her at the drop of a hat! It makes my blood run cold just thinking about it!

MUM *(sitting down)* You're mixing up Canada with those movies that Nelson Eddy and Jeanette MacDonald made.

NORAH enters with the calendar, followed by SHEILAH.

Norah, show your Aunt Girlie what Canada really looks like.

NORAH See, *(showing her a calendar)* this is where I'm going to live, Aunt Girlie.

SHEILAH goes to fiddle with a sprig of flowers which she is trying to attach to a hat.

GIRLIE London Life?

NORAH It's where Ben's father works. He's an insurance agent. It's ever such a big company.

MUM That's their new office building...right in the middle of the town...I don't see any log huts, Girlie.

HARRY Isn't that impressive, now, Girlie?

MUM Did you bring the letter too?

NORAH Yes, right here.

MUM It's from Ben's mother...doesn't she have a lovely hand?

IVY enters from the kitchen with a hat veil.

SHEILAH Help me with these flowers, you two. *(trying on her hat)* I'm about ready to chuck them in the dust bin.

IVY *(placing them for her)* How about here, then?

SHEILAH Oh...no...try the other side?

GIRLIE Well...*(looking up from the letter)* she sounds all right, but, of course, you can't really judge by a letter, Maggie.

HARRY I'd say they seem like a very nice family. Very kind.

GIRLIE She says she sent the rings? Nooie, aren't you going to show me the rings, then?

IVY Here we go.

NORAH Oh, *(going to the sideboard)* I took my engagement ring off while I was cleaning Mum's shoes.

NORAH takes the ring to GIRLIE.

GIRLIE *(rummaging in her handbag)* Drat it...*(bringing out a weird assortment)* Where is that thing? *(she finds a jeweller's loupe, spits on her handkerchief and cleans the glass)* Now, Nooie...let's have a look at that diamond.

NORAH I know it's not large, Aunt Girlie, but it's set in platinum.

Once GIRLIE puts the loupe to her eye, HARRY picks up his 'mac', taps IVY on the shoulder, and they moves upstage, where he unloads one bottle of scotch, and bottle of gin and two bottles of sherry. IVY sneaks them into the sideboard.

GIRLIE *(once the business is finished)* It's not much bigger than a chip...still it's a good blue...yes, it's all right. *(general reaction of disbelief that she's said something nice)* Where's your wedding ring?

SHEILAH brings a purple velvet ring box.

SHEILAH Don't you think it's lovely?

GIRLIE Lovely box, anyway.

NORAH And the ring's so dainty.

GIRLIE Yes, but the value's in the weight, Nooie. It's very light. Still if you like it...

NORAH *(slipping the engagement ring on her finger and holding out her hand)* Uncle Harry...

GIRLIE Good heavens, Nooie! Your hands are all green!

SHEILAH Not green. Turquoise. It's turquoise dye.

NORAH I was dyeing some white gloves to go with my suit.

IVY We've tried everything to get it off, but nothing works.

GIRLIE Oh, nothing does anything to dye. And it'll take weeks to wear off.

MUM What's a bit of green anyway? A blind man would—

HARRY and the GIRLS join in to finish the phrase.

— be glad to see it.

SHEILAH And if you'll excuse us, Mum, Norah and I have something to do upstairs.

GIRLIE *(getting up)* It's time we were movin'—

NORAH I'll see you tomorrow. Uncle Harry, don't forget you're giving me away.

HARRY I could hardly forget that, Nooie.

The GIRLS exit giggling.

HARRY She's all aglow, isn't she?

MUM She's going to be heart-broken I'm afraid.

HARRY Now, Maggie...

GIRLIE She won't be the only one. After me spending a small fortune on a new dress.

HARRY Girlie...

GIRLIE A lovely satin, Maggie...

HARRY Not now, Girlie.

GIRLIE Peacock blue.

MUM Peacock blue. Well, Girlie, that will suit you to a T.

IVY And I suppose you'll wear your fur coat, too, Aunt Girlie?

GIRLIE I was intending to, Ivy.

HARRY Maggie...

GIRLIE You can't trust the weather in June, you know. Maggie, you tell Nooie she's not to send back these rings.

HARRY Maggie, I—

GIRLIE She should get some bit of good out of being left at the altar. Dinger! Come on!

HARRY *(ignoring GIRLIE)* What I'm trying to tell you is... don't be too sure Norah's going to be disappointed. Even if the Second Front is started any day now, the High Command won't want the Germans to know exactly which day. So it stands to reason that all leave won't be cancelled.

MUM Really, Harry?

HARRY It'd be too easy a tip off for old Hitler. It's possible that Ben may be one of the lucky ones.

MUM It's a slim chance, though, isn't it?

HARRY Well, suppose the invasion does cancel his leave, the wedding will just be postponed 'til he comes back, won't it?

MUM *If* he comes back, Harry.

GIRLIE Red with blood the English channel will be! Red with—

HARRY Girlie. Shut-up!

GIRLIE is left with her mouth wide open. He stands and takes her by the arm.

We'll see ourselves out, Maggie. You and Norah just keep your fingers crossed.

HARRY propels a dumbstruck GIRLIE out. IVY and MUM look at each other in disbelief.

MUM That's more like the Harry I used to know.

SHEILAH *(coming downstairs, preceding NORAH into the room)* Ta-dah!

NORAH enters in wedding dress and walks slowly up to her mother.

MUM Oh, Norah...you're a picture...

SHEILAH I told you Mum would get all weepy.

NORAH They're tears of joy, aren't they, Mum?

MUM nods.

NORAH Sheilah, I've you to thank for this. My white wedding...but I think the parachute was meant for you, wasn't it?

SHEILAH *(shrugs)* Charlie said there were a few oil spots...But I see Mrs. Redman has managed to cut round them. *(pointing to a spot)* Oh, here's one.

MUM A man wouldn't get off—

All three GIRLS join in.

GIRLS — a galloping horse to look at that.

SHEILAH Norah, why don't you model what you're going to wear tomorrow night?

NORAH My flannelette pyjamas?

SHEILAH You don't mean you spent all those coupons without saving any for the most important thing?

MUM Hang on...*(going to the side cupboard and taking out a parcel)* I don't know where my mind is these days. *(as NORAH opens it)* Madge sent it down.

NORAH It's a nightgown. *(she holds up a modest pink night-gown)* It's pink.

IVY We can see that.

NORAH Oh, I like the puff sleeves. It's very nice.

SHEILAH Nice? For a honeymoon you don't want nice. You want "Wicked." Red! or Black! And see-through!

IVY slips over to the sideboard.

MUM Sheilah! Wherever do you get such ideas?

SHEILAH Rita Hayworth wore one like that in a film I saw.

MUM Rita Hayworth indeed. Norah, I can guarantee you that nightgown is practically new...Madge only wore it in the hospital when she had Roy.

SHEILAH Do you suppose she was wearing it when she was in labour? How romantic.

MUM Times like these we all have to make sacrifices.

SHEILAH *(to IVY)* After all, she won't have it on for long.

MUM What was that, Sheilah?

SHEILAH I said, after all, there's a war on.

MUM gives her a long look.

IVY I've something too. *(handing NORAH a small, gift-wrapped present)* I know I've been a bit of a wet blanket about your wedding, but — I really do hope you'll be very happy.

NORAH I know you do, Ivy.

She opens the parcel and holds aloft a pair of stockings.

Are they...can't be...nylon stockings? Oh, Ivy! However did you get hold of them?

SHEILAH I think it would be best not to ask, in case Ivy incriminates herself!

MUM *(worried)* They aren't...black market, are they, Ivy?

IVY No Mum! Don't worry! I was lucky, that's all...

SHEILAH That's a bit vague, Ivy! *Do* tell us who you were "ever so nice" to! *(miming looking into a crystal ball)* Ah...I'm getting a picture...It's a GI..he's on crutches.

IVY Your crystal ball's a bit behind the times. He's not on crutches anymore. He's "in the swing" these days.

NORAH Oh, that's why you're looking so "hep".

IVY Isn't it time we cleared the table off?

MUM High time, I'd say.

IVY and SHEILAH start piling things on trays. NORAH moves to join them.

MUM *(to NORAH)* Not you, not in your dress.

NORAH I'll get changed.

IVY and SHEILAH exit to the kitchen.

MUM Norah, before you go...*(as NORAH turns back, she passes her a small envelope)* It's not a present exactly — I just thought you might...oh, here.

NORAH *(opening the envelope and taking out a small picture torn into two pieces)* My father...?

MUM *(nodding)* When he left, I thought I didn't want anything to remind me of him, so I...well, you can see. I tried to throw it away, but I couldn't. It was the only picture I had of him, so I just hid it away. It's only since you made me talk about him that night...well, I've come to realize he and I...we were ...casualties of the war...no different to thousands of others. *(beat)* I was going to try to glue it back together, but I thought...well, you'd do a better job, wouldn't you?

They embrace silently. IVY comes back in, and stops in the doorway.

MUM Now, go change your dress.

NORAH runs upstairs, IVY wipes the table.

IVY *(to MUM)* Supposing Ben doesn't come, how long are we going to wait before we do something about it?

MUM I suppose we should warn the relatives.

SHEILAH comes in.

IVY And cancel the restaurant and the florist. I can go round to Uncle Harry's club on my bike. There's a phone there.

MUM I think the vicar should be told personally.

SHEILAH We're giving up hope, then, are we?

IVY He'd be here by now if he'd got leave. Or at least phoned!

SHEILAH He might not be able to...if he was on a train, for instance.

IVY Sheilah, I want Norah to have her wedding just as much as you do...

SHEILAH I asked Charlie to come. He said he might.

IVY Oh?

MUM *(pause)* Funny, we were all so against her getting married. We have to face facts. It doesn't look like he's coming.

SHEILAH Poor Norah...

IVY Maybe we could wait another half hour.

MUM Well...why don't you find a good programme on the wireless? Take Norah's mind off waiting. And I'll make some cocoa.

IVY Where's the *Radio Times*?

SHEILAH There's never anything on a Sunday night except church services.

MUM They sing some lovely old hymns.

SHEILAH Oh, marvellous.

MUM *(with the radio times)* There's a very entertaining programme on tonight, so you can stop your sniggering. Music from the Palm Court. From right here in Bournemouth. You know, Albert Sandler and his violin. *(The GIRLS look puzzled)* You know — the one who does the canary on his violin. All those little trills. Tweet tweet tweet.

IVY Tweet tweet tweet?

NORAH comes down.

MUM Oh, Norah...Albert Sandler is on the wireless tonight. We're all in for a treat.

SHEILAH Cocoa and canaries.

NORAH You'll have to count me out when Ben arrives.

MUM Yes, of course.

IVY Of course, Norah.

NORAH You don't think he's coming. I can see it in your faces.

MUM Norah, we hope he is, but...*(she looks at the girls for support)*

SHEILAH Come on, our Norah! If there is something big, like the Second Front going on, do you think Eisenhower and Monty and all that lot are going to say, "Let's leave it for a bit. There's this girl in Bournemouth

SHEILAH *(continued)* who's getting married to one of our troops right now!"

IVY Winston Churchill wouldn't like it!

NORAH *(managing a faint smile)* You're right. I'm sorry. It's just...it's like that thing we used to skip to. "When will he marry me, will he ever, this year, next year, sometime, never." I was always out on "never."

There is another silence.

SHEILAH *(getting up)* Oh, for heavens' sake! Let's have Albert Sandler.

They put the wireless on and hear 'Tweet tweet tweet'. They listen to tweets and trills for a few bars, laughing.

NORAH *(in a whisper)* Oh Mum!

There is dead silence as they follow her eyes. We see a soldier with full kit pause outside the window. NORAH is motionless for a moment, then with a little cry she is out of her chair, and into the kitchen. The soldier puts down his kit bag and straightens his cap and uniform jacket. And we see NORAH fly into his arms. MUM and the GIRLS are riveted to their seats. Through the window we see NORAH and BEN embrace.

MUM *(wiping away a tear)* Oh! Thank God!

IVY is also teary-eyed.

SHEILAH *(she sighs, then a thought hits her)* She'll get to wear the nightgown after all!

SHEILAH is shushed simultaneously by MUM and IVY.

SHEILAH Oh, I give up! You'd better not be all soft and soppy like this when me and Charlie get married!

MUM *(dismay and shock on her face)* Not you too. Dear Lord!

IVY *(disbelieving)* You're kidding!

SHEILAH You'll see! But don't worry Mum — I won't be stealing your Typhoo Tips for my wedding outfit! I've already got enough coupons for what I want!

IVY looks at her questioningly.

SHEILAH *(wickedly)* A black chiffon nightgown!

Music swells and the stage fades to black.

The End.